Windows 10: From Beginner to Expert:

A Complete User Guide to Microsoft's Optimized and Intelligent New Operating System

Nick Goddard

Legal & Disclaimer

Legal & Disclaimer

The information contained in this book is not designed to replace or take the place of any form of medicine or professional medical advice. The information in this book has been provided for educational and entertainment purposes only.

Table of Contents

Windows 10: From Beginner to Expert:

A Complete User Guide to Microsoft's Optimized and Intelligent New Operating System

Introduction

Users are used to the old set up of Start menu button provided in Windows 7. When the button disappeared in Windows 8, it created confusion, and many users started complaining about its disappearance from the OS. However, Microsoft took heed from it and brought it back with the latest Windows version. The Win 10 is all about user convenience, so that users on XP and 8.1 will be able to adjust to the upgrade. Additionally, the latest version is a bit similar in its working with the tile mix that helps retain some part of its predecessor.

Universal apps

The Windows Store apps, when displayed on existing Windows versions would occupy the entire screen. It hampered the productivity of the users by making multi-tasking difficult. With the latest version of Windows, Microsoft made it possible for users to increase productivity. The ability to create virtual desktops is an amazing addition.

Personalization

Windows 8 tile layout meant big icons that were supposed to make things simpler. Using the Start screen a user could arrange and resize tiles. The ease of functionality and the UI utility were enough to convince users to invest in the OS. Nonetheless, many users still missed upon the convenience served by traditional desktop. With the launch of Windows 10, the traditional as well as modern OS were utilized to create an interesting mix. Elements of both the versions are incorporated that makes the upcoming OS configurable. You can easily move or pin applications to the menu as per your convenience.

One platform

The basic functionality and shared apps on Windows 10 are available across any platform. It is more about being able to provide one platform experience to the users. It is all about selling the idea of making this latest OS version an intuitive UI that changes according to the environment it is used with or on the device a user would use it.

Desktop management

The Mac OS X and Linux were the first to incorporate the technology of multiple-desktops. Now, Microsoft too seems to have joined the bandwagon. With the inclusion of Start screen, the Win 8 was working on single point focus. However, with its proposed successor the ability of making changes in the desktop environments is included for user convenience. The ability to access a screen from another screen, even from Windows Store applications is a great way to incorporate desktop management.

Task View

The feature of Task View helps you work with applications and processes on multiple desktops. This feature makes it easier for any user to continue working with ease. The full screen on Windows 8 was not helping user in multi-tasking. The Task View along with the Snap Assist feature generated preview of all the current Windows in one go. You will be able to see all the windows along with an app within a single screen. Working is made easy with paired application to organize your work.

The above-mentioned are some of the key differences that set apart the two versions of the OS. Let us hope that the latest Windows version fulfills the expectations of the users.

Xx Essential Programs for Windows 10

Listing of essential programs (most open source and / or platform) with tips and tricks in everyday desktop use, you help us to complete the list?

Throughout the years using Windows, we got used to using certain applications that make our life easier and more comfortable. Taking advantage of the recent release of Windows 10 want to throw a simple question to my readers: What are your essential applications to use Windows?

Installation Options for Windows 10

Regardless of whether your computer is a Mac or a PC, or you want to install on your current version, in a different partition or through a virtual machine, you will find all the answers here.

Requirements for installing Windows 10

Windows 10 is not a system that requires a powerful machine. It is true that more power will result in a better experience, but you see, the minimum requirements are quite affordable:

Processor at 1GHz or faster

1GB of RAM for 32-bit version and 2GB for 64-bit

16GB of free disk space. If we create a partition, you must have at least 45GB in total

Graphics card compatible with Microsoft DirectX 9 with WDDM driver

Microsoft account and internet access

I think you will agree they are not anything special. Any computer with Windows 8.1 can run without problems Windows 10. Even older computers that came with Windows Vista will also make the leap.

But the best thing is that thanks to these requirements you can also use virtualization to install Windows 10 without worrying that you will screw up your current installation or ride "playing" with disk partitions.

How to Get Windows 10

Before you begin, you must first learn how to get the latest version of Windows 10 from their official site or secondary resellers.

Of course, you have to choose the appropriate language and then release: x86 or x64. If you have a computer with 32-bit processor will have to opt for the ISO x86, but if you have a 64-bit then x64 suits you better.

Installing Windows 10

Installing Windows 10 is something that can be done in several ways namely: installing from scratch on a new partition, updating your system (here you can choose to save data or not) or resort to using VMs.

Upgrading to Windows 10

Choosing to upgrade to Windows 10 is the easiest process. If you access the web from your Windows PC, Windows will give you an option to download the necessary files for an upgrade. You can also do it if you have already downloaded the ISO and burned it on a DVD.

In both cases you will see a wizard that will give you the

option to choose whether to keep or delete the data.

Once you choose your option it will be a matter of waiting

a few minutes for the whole process to complete.

INSTALLATION FROM SCRATCH

Windows-10-install

Like I said, Windows 10 is still in its early stages, that

means you can install version right now will have many

more added features in the future. That is why, if you're going to use it in your work machine, you should be careful.

To avoid problems do not touch your current installation, install on a new partition or disk from scratch. This option is not complicated but it is not always possible. First because you cannot have more bays for additional disks and, secondly, there is a risk in creating new partitions.

Therefore, if you have knowledge to manage new partitions my advice it is to skip to the next option: virtualization.

Virtualizing Windows 10

With the power offered by the current computers, virtualizing an operating system is not only possible but one of the best options if you are unafraid to test a system in development. True, you will not get the best performance but will get to enjoy major features.

To virtualize Windows 10, make use of virtualization applications like Parallels, VMware Fusion or VirtualBox . Integration and performance for the first two options would be the most desirable but VirtualBox provides a huge advantage, it is free.

Therefore, I will use VirtualBox to explain what the process of creating and installing Windows 10 on a virtual machine.

Virtual Box 1

Download and install the application, choose the option to create a new virtual machine name and select assign version: Windows 10 (64-bit). From there you set the RAM: if you have more than 4GB intended to be more than 2GB set number. In my case, I have 8GB of physical RAM, I chose to assign to the virtual machine 4GB.

Virtual Box 2

Now it's just a matter of selecting our Windows 10 image and performing the installation process, which has no differences from doing so in a partition on the hard drive on your computer.

Now that you know how to install Windows 10, I wish to remind you a few details. This whole process may seem suitable only to PC users but is not. If you have a Mac you will be able to install Windows 10 and test its offering over OS X.

In case you have a Mac and want to try Windows 10, my recommendation is to use virtualization. Although apple officially supports windows 10 via bootcamp.

So go ahead, download, install and test Windows 10. Shortly after starting to use the system you will notice that something is changing in Microsoft. They are doing many things well and Windows 10 is one of them, especially in the wake of future integration with mobile devices.

How to Upgrade to Windows 10? Guide Questions and Answers

Microsoft is free since 29 July, the latest version of its operating system. Should you make copies of photos and music? What functions will be lost? A guide to a smooth upgrade

Since Microsoft offered to reserve a copy of Windows 10 to users of legal versions 7 and 8.1, consultations on migration have considerably increased because many times users have in their hands the daunting task of upgrading the operating system on their computers for the first time.

How do I reserve my copy of Windows 10?

Months ago Microsoft began offering backup Windows 10 users with compatible equipment. Through an icon in the bottom bar of the computer desk you can access to the option that provides for the upgrade.

Why don't I see the invitation to upgrade?

The most common explanation is that you PC does not use the original version of Windows 7 or 8.1.

It is also possible that Windows Update is not configured to receive updates automatically. If that's the case, you must enable the option to receive the invitation.

What are the requirements for my computer to upgrade?

The arrival of the invitation to upgrade to Windows 10 generally means that the equipment is compatible.

If the user wants to remove his doubts, you can verify himself. In the invitation to try Windows 10 there is the option of scanning your computer to find out.

Here is the list of features that should have a computer to run the system:

-Processor: 1GHz or higher

-RAM: 1GB to 2GB for 32-bit or 64-bit

-Space on the hard drive: 16GB to 20GB for 32-bit or 64-bit

-Credit Graph: DirectX 9 with WDDM 1.0 or higher driver

-Display: 1024 × 600

What will be the price of Windows 10?

For a year, downloading Windows 10 will be free for users who currently use Windows 7, Windows 8.1 and Windows Phone 8.1. That license is irrevocable. As of July 29, 2016, who have not made the download must pay S119 for the Home version u $ 199 for the Pro version.

How do I upgrade if I have Windows XP, Vista or RT?

In that case, the only option for you to get Windows 10 will be by paying for a copy.

Another possibility, which is very annoying for most, is to be registered in the Windows Insider program, i.e. in the group of users that test improvements to be done on Windows 10. This means that the computer can become unstable or present failures. If you opt out of the program, Microsoft forces the user to return to XP or Vista, depending on the operating system you had before enrolling.

Windows RT users will upgrade to Windows 10 a bit later.

What version of Windows 10 I get?

Users of Windows 7 Starter, Home Basic and Home Premium will receive Windows 10 Home. Those with

Windows 7 Professional or Ultimate will receive Windows 10 Pro.

Users with Windows 8.1 to Windows 10 Home will and those with Pro 8.1 and Pro 8.1 for Students see that their equipment will be upgraded to Windows 10 Pro.

Computers with Windows Phone 8.1 to Windows 10 will Mobile. This will not happen later, but could soon when Microsoft ends agreeing with phone companies upgrade.

Is it difficult to update? Can I do it myself?

Microsoft sought to make the process of upgrading to Windows 10 as simple as possible.

While it is always advisable to keep a backup of the files stored on the computer, the company promised that photos, music, documents, videos and others will be safe during the process of upgrading to Windows 10. The same goes for the settings.

If the computer on which the upgrade is done takes time working or is overloaded with files, it is best to clean documents first, save them on a disc, and let Windows 10 start virtually from scratch.

Can I go back to my previous operating system?

Yes. The option of returning to Windows 8.1 or 7 will be available for one month.

Does the copy of Windows 10 get lost in case of formatting?

No. The operating system license will be associated with the machine, so that you can reinstall Windows 10 as often as you desire on the same computer.

How long does it take to install the update?

Downloading Windows 10 is automatic and the time it takes will depend on the quality of Internet connection.

Once the download is complete, the system will alert you, notifying you that the installation is ready to begin. Newer devices may take up to 20 minutes to complete the installation and the older ones over an hour.

What functions are lost with Windows 10?

In Windows 10 Media Center, found in Windows 7 Home Premium, Windows 7 Professional, Windows 7 Ultimate, Windows 8 Pro and Windows 8.1 Pro Disappears.

For DVD playback you will require a separate software.

The Windows 7desktop gadgets will be removed as part of the Windows 10 installation.

Users of Windows 10 Home are derived of the updates on Windows Update automatically.

The Solitaire, Minesweeper and Hearts games that come pre-installed in Windows 7, are disposed as part of the installation of the upgrade to Windows 10. Microsoft launched their own versions of Solitaire and Minesweeper, called "Microsoft Solitaire Collection" and " Microsoft Minesweeper ". They are downloaded from the Store.

If you have a USB floppy drive, you must download the latest driver from Windows Update or the manufacturer's website.

If you have Windows Live Essentials installed on the system, the application will be removed.

And with Internet Explorer?

The default browser in Windows 10 is the Microsoft Edge which is far superior to any of previous versions of IE in Microsoft's browser history. Clean design and ability to take notes are its two key characteristics.

Is it mandatory to upgrade?

No, but worth trying Windows 10. In addition to the return of the Start button with an improved menu,

Microsoft achieved a unique interaction between Windows and Xbox, including application store for all devices in your system.

In addition to this is the new Edge browser, Internet Explorer replacement, the possibility to work with up to four applications on the screen and create virtual desktops, a feature that is only now landing in Windows.

In addition, Windows 10 is free and will "revive" old machines.

Windows 10 Configuration to Protect Privacy

Windows 10 has some new useful features, but if you think what this means rest of the Internet world out the waiting to pounce on your connected world, this could also come increased vulnerability. However, this idea is somewhat exaggerated. Let's look at what each element of the privacy settings is and what it really does, and which ones pose a risk. Windows 10 you have the reputation of being some sort of " home phone " more than its predecessors. It is true, but most of this behavior is already in Windows 8, and can also be found on it on Android, iOS and Chrome. Of course, that does not mean that all functions are recommended. Simply, there is nothing new under the sun. Many security experts have published a list of the settings that you must disable in

Windows 10 to protect your privacy, but most do not explain in detail what makes each of these settings risky, what this does is to make it difficult to separate facts from fiction. Here I offer to walk you through these settings, what I know about what they are and the actual repercussions of disabling them.

General Settings Privacy

Let's start with the obvious. Open the Windows 10 settings and go to Privacy> General. Most of the settings in this section are self-explanatory, but here's what they do:

They allow applications to use my id. Advertising: This helps Microsoft to offer you more personalized ads in applications that support them. You can disable it without affecting your user experience.

Activate the filter Smartscreen: This sends the addresses within the Windows Store if you buy from Microsoft to verify that you are not in a list of malicious sites and applications. Google does the same thing, but locally, that is, with the list on your own computer, and only sends the URLs if we activated the option to share usage statistics. I think it's a very useful function, so I normally leave it on. Note that this only affects the way we visit sites in other apps different to Edge browser. Below I will explain how to activate and deactivate Edge.

Send information to Microsoft about how to write: This function allows you to improve auto-suggestions. It is supposed to be for what we write on the keyboard, or with the manual writing on touchscreens.

Let websites offering relevant local content: If you speak another language other than English, this feature could be useful. Feel free to turn it off.

In short, you can disable all these settings and not notice any striking difference. Additionally, you can use the free application for Windows 10 DoNotSpy allowing 37 points off privacy with just one click.

In Windows 10, just like iOS or Android, you can use your location to provide better user experience in certain applications, for example, you can check your location so you do not have to enter your zip code every time you look at what the weather is in your neighborhood, or to show where you are on the maps. However, you are likely to have to share your location with a number of trusted partners such as meteorological service. In a normal desktop computer, this will probably not bring much advantage as it does to a mobile device such as a tablet or a smartphone, you can disable this entirely if you prefer. You only go to: Settings> Privacy> Location and view the list of applications on the bottom. You can disable applications individually, or completely disable this feature above. Just keep in mind that the general location needs to be active or Cortana will not work.

Cortana and start menu search

Cortana has some of the tightest privacy functions, but is also one of the most useful features of the new Windows, this means you have to decide between your privacy or part of that utility. To work, Cortana records your voice (to understand what you say), your location (to adjust the answers to where you are), you write (to answer), contacts (so you can refer to them), the events of your calendar (to create, edit, or give information about them), and more. That's a lot of privacy. Of course, not much different from Siri or Google Now, which also collect a lot of data (on your smartphone instead of the PC).

Fortunately, like those other attendees, Cortana is easy to

disable if you want an iron privacy. To do that you must change the following options:

Disable Cortana: Open the Start menu and type something. Click on the notepad icon on the left side and select Settings. From there you can disable and Cortana.

Search online and web results include: When you turn off Cortana, this option will appear. You can disable it if you do not want to make any suggestion from the start menu, which also records what you type and sends it to Microsoft for their predictions automatically. Exactly the same as Google.com, Chrome or Firefox.

Get to know me: In Settings> Privacy> Voice input handwritten script is a function called Get to know me.

This is probably the feature that most violates the privacy of all Windows 10. Even after disabling Cortana, you must do the same with this function. Just press the Stop button to achieve this.

Manage cloud information: You need to know how Windows 10 makes stores your data on your computer, deleting a local file solves the problem most of the time but you have to delete the copy in the cloud separately. In the same window, click Go to Bing and manages personal information on all your devices to delete data stored your Microsoft account.

Sending information to Microsoft explained above is the major privacy concern Windows 10. Much of the reason is that they use such vague language that specifies how and when to they use you data, say, what you are writing. That is very problematic.

This is the type of function that users can disable at any time. Microsoft does not collect personal information through this feature. What is collected is only for process improvement purposes. For example, to improve the handwriting to text translation engine, or to enrich the Windows dictionary and spelling functions. The data goes through a rigorous multiple filter to ensure what is collected is not identifiable information or sensitive data such as email addresses, passwords or alphanumeric codes. Then, the collected data is fragmented into very small sequences so that they can be reconstructed to form an identifiable whole. Samples of collected data are limited. Microsoft does not capture everything you write, or do it all the time.

In short, it is not a Keylogger program. More like a text analysis software that select parts of a sequence and analyzes it for the purpose of self-correction and dictionary. However, once again, the concept of privacy is extremely broad, and the function remains worrying from the user's point of view. If you are concerned about this issue and you prefer to live without Cortana, you just can just turn it off.

Microsoft Edge

This is the new Microsoft browser, like most of the new browsers (and that includes Chrome and Firefox) it includes some features that modernize you browsing experience. Go to: Settings> Advanced Settings. To change any if its settings

Cortana and Microsoft Edge: If you are using Cortana, it will track your browsing history to use it as a reference when you ask things. You can disable it if you want.

Show search suggestions when writing: Like the Start menu, Edge records what you type, but it does to offer predictive text. If you do not want it just turn it off.

Protect my PC against malicious sites and downloads: As we mentioned in the first section, the SmartScreen Filter can register Web addresses you've visited to try to protect against malicious sites. I recommend leaving it turned on, but if you want to disable it, no one will stop you.

If you do not use Microsoft Edge, these settings matter less, but it's always nice to know where they are.

Synchronize Windows settings

Many features of Windows 10 require a Microsoft account and this data is stored in the cloud or synchronized via the Internet. The most important data privacy are:

Sync settings: In Settings> Accounts> Sync settings can decide to share with your other PCs with Windows 10. This includes your desktop wallpaper and theme your browser settings, passwords, accessibility and more. You can disable it here.

BitLocker encryption: Encrypts your hard drive. To do this, BitLocker comes pre-installed on all versions of Windows 10. However, if you have the Home Edition, it will automatically store your recovery key with your Microsoft account. There is not much you can do about it except get a Windows 10 Pro for more security features or use an alternative encryption program such as VeraCrypt .

Optionally, you can avoid using a Microsoft account by using a local account during installation, or getting into Settings> Accounts> Your Account and picking the local account option. If you do, note that you cannot download apps from the Windows Store or use many of its functions mentioned above.

Comments and diagnostics

Like many other applications and operating systems, Microsoft can send diagnostic data to help troubleshoot your computer. This option also sends information inadvertently. Perhaps you prefer not to call many memory registers or the apps you use most often. If you go into Settings> Privacy> Comments and diagnostics, you'll see the two points to consider:

Frequency: Occasionally, Windows 10 will ask you your opinion about the system. If you do not want to bother with it simply select Never.

Diagnosis and use of data: This function can send a lot of information to Microsoft, including how often you use certain applications, which ones you use most often, or capture fragments of a document you're working during a crash. You can change the degree to which it does. You have more information about each one here.

Microsoft does not allow completely disable diagnostic except in Enterprise versions of Windows 10. The basic level of this tool only works with data that is crucial to the operation of Windows, as updates or protection against malicious software.

Manage WiFi Connections

Windows 10 includes a new feature called WiFi sense that allows us to connect to WiFi networks without a password protected making it through Facebook, Outlook or Skype from a friend. In this way, we can automatically connect to the WiFi network from a friend without asking for the password. It is safer to share key access, since your friend can not share that connection. Most of the process is optional, so you should not worry too much about it. You have to activate a check box to share the WiFi network with your contacts, and they have to do the same. However, you can make your WiFi network not to be shared in this way if you add "_optout" at the end of the SSID address. By default, Windows will give the option to connect to networks that your friends have shared with you. If you want to disable it, you can make in Settings> Network and Internet> Wi-Fi> Manage WiFi settings.

Windows updates

Unlike its predecessors, Windows 10 does not offer the ability to disable the updates. Users of Windows 10 Pro, Enterprise and Education have that option through the registration group, but Home editions cannot disable it. This is due to safety reasons, so I do not recommend deactivating. You can always disable specific patches though.

Windows Update also uses a file system share the BitTorrent protocol update information. That's fine, but if you do not want other people to download updates using your bandwidth, you can disable the option: Settings> Updates and Security> Advanced> Updates

Choose how you want the updates delivered.

On this screen, disable, or better yet change the radio button to include only computers on your local network. This will allow your network equipment upgrade faster, but close access to other Internet users.

Is the Windows 10 operating system Privacy killer in history?

Probably not, but it has its problems. Mainly:

Descriptions of some of the settings are very vague, making it difficult to know when your data is collected or what type of data collected. How to know the function is probably the most insidious in this regard.

All options are opt-out rather than opt-in. In other words, they are enabled by default and you have to disable them. Most users will never dive so deep in the configuration. Al least, Microsoft offers the ability to set more or less everything to our liking, a step in the right direction. Apart from these problems, there is nothing that we've talked it particularly new. Criminalizing the start menu because it offers predictive text seems a bit out of place, especially when we have been use that same technology in Google.com, Chrome and Firefox for years. Most functions also exist in other operating systems and, of course, on your smartphone.

This does not mean you should stop worrying about privacy. It is a personal decision. If you feel uncomfortable with any of the above settings here, or if you do not trust what Microsoft does with the data, simply disable them, but beware you have to sacrifice certain new features. Just be aware that Microsoft is far from being the only company that does this, so be sure to check your privacy settings in other applications or operating systems (such as the browser or OSX). The only way to protect all your data is by disconnecting to the Internet.

Guide to Windows 10 Backup: Backup, Restore and Recovery

The backup is an essential maintenance task for anyone seeking to protect personal and corporate information on a computer. The stakes are high. Losing forever those photographs that portrayed an unforgettable moment or professionals who have career defining documents stored on their PCs is not an option.

Losing those files is easier than you think. Malware infection is the order of the day and a simple ramsonware Trojan can cause data loss or operating system corruption generally caused by an application or driver installation. On the other hand, no team is safe from physical failure of the storage unit which can prevent access to the unit and the computer.

That is why backups are essential, achievable task from powerful business solutions and also from the same operating system. Today we review the possibilities of Windows 10 Backup , performing backup and restoration , and options system recovery , which will return the system to an earlier point before the problems began.

Full Backup System

It is the right approach when we want to preserve all computer data, operating system, configuration, applications and user files . The tool will create a complete image can be restored in case of critical errors in it. With this step by step:

Access the control panel menu system from Windows 10 user (right click on the start button)

Click on Backup and Restore (Windows 7)

Click on Create a system image

Choose where the image is saved on a hard disk or flash drive, optical disc DVD or a network drive

Confirm and start the process by clicking Start Backup

Backup_Windows10_2

The backup may take from 10 minutes to several hours depending on the amount of data to be processed even if the computer can be used normally during the process. The tool does not allow customization files to include but is a simple method realizable from the same operating system, which will produce us a complete picture of the system can be restored in case of problems.

Backup files

It is the method indicated to save a backup file to recover if lost or damaged.

Access the Control Panel System

Click on File history

Connect an external drive as a hard drive or USB flash drive or choose a network drive

If you have several select the drive to use for the file history

Click on the button Activate

The tool saved files Libraries, Desktop, and Favorites

Contact

If you do not want to keep specific folders and libraries

can add exclusions in paragraph

BackupWindows10

An active time for the first time, you can access the

Advanced Settings to choose how often the copies and

the time saved versions will remain will be made. In case

of problems you only have to click on the option Restore

personal files and choose the version of the files you

want to restore to its original location.

Advanced Recovery

Complementing the above options Backup and Restore, Windows 10 also offers advanced recovery tool that ungoes changes made to the system reverting the computer to a previous restore point . Very useful in case of problems with the installation of a driver or application that prevents the normal functioning of the operating system. To activate:

Access the Control Panel System

Click on Recovery

Click on Set System Restore

Active protection system and disk space usage by clicking Set

Create a restore point system

Backup_Windows10_3

From here you will automatically create restore points. As you fill the space chosen for the protection of the system will be phased out previous restore points. To return to an earlier point in the same tool provides the function to restore the system and correct problems . System Restore does not affect documents, images or other personal data.

Creating a recovery unit

The above tool also provides the ability to create a recovery unit to use when the computer can not start or in case of problems. As follows:

Access the Control Panel System

Click on Recovery

Click on Create a recovery unit

The external drive used must be at least 8 Gigabytes of free space. (All data will be removed from this unit)

BackupWindows10_2

Once created we can use it to access the computer and troubleshooting. If we use the option Backup system files, we can also use it to reinstall Windows if necessary.

Do not leave for tomorrow. "Spending a" making these backups and recovery time Windows 10 is a future investment that can save your life in case of problems. If a replacement of damaged hardware can be solved, loss of business or personal files can have a high cost and sometimes without possible recovery. The recovery tool is another essential feature that allows you to return your computer to an earlier point in a simple and fast as we had before the trouble started, thereby saving valuable

time in your operating system installation, configuration,

applications and data.

How is the Security of the New Windows 10

Windows 10 is arguably one of the most anticipated operating systems ever introduced by Microsoft, it is also considered to be one of the most critical of OS releases. But, does it actually live up to its promises when it comes to things like security? Well, we have attempted to apply our powerful brain to find the details on how Windows 10 does in the security department.

Device Guard

According to recent technology, the new Device Guard feature works by blocking all zero day attacks by vetting the apps which attempt to access a Windows 10 device or its network. In other words, Device Guard can block any application that is not signed by an authentic software vendor or the Windows app store of an enterprise.

The new feature is available on all devices working on the Windows 10 OS, for instance, Acer, HP, Toshiba, Lenovo and NCR. It also supports IoT type devices, which run Windows, ATM machines and POS systems, providing a first layer of security across the board.

Device Guard is also able to use hardware technology along with virtualization to isolate the decision making process from the rest of the OS, consequently helping it provide protection from all sorts of malware threats that have somehow managed to gain access to system privileges.

App control technologies and other traditional anti-virus software will depend on this feature to help block executable malware threats while the anti-virus will continue to cover the areas that are outside Device Guard territory. For instance, Java based apps or macros in documents. Furthermore, Device Guard operates virtually so even if a Windows kernel is infected, the Device Guard feature is still able to remain safe.

The "Passport" Feature

Another useful security feature in the new Windows 10 OS is the Passport feature that allows users to authenticate network sans passwords, applications and websites. How this works is, the operating system will ask the user to verify that they are in possession of their device before authenticating it for the user either with a PIN code or with the use of biometric sensors.

Once a device has been authenticated through Passport, the user will be allowed access to a huge set of websites and services, from social networking sites to business networks and much more. Furthermore, Microsoft has also been making some changes to its OS with the help of containers and virtualized sandboxes to make desktop computers more secure.

Windows Hello

Microsoft as the eventual killer of the password has boasted this feature, mainly because it uses biometrics to secure a Windows 10 powered system. In other words, the technology uses your fingerprint, face and iris to launch a Windows 10 powered device rather than the conventional password that we are all so used to.

According to Joe Belfiore, corporate VP at Microsoft, the use of newest technology, such as biometrics makes the Windows 10 operating system more secure than its predecessors and keeps the user safe from the vulnerabilities of passwords. It also gives users the ability to authenticate various Windows 10 applications and their online experience without having to provide a password on a network server or a user's device.

The only catch here is that a user will need to have a device that has a fingerprint reader and the required scanning software to identify a user by using their face or iris. Also, these features will require the user to have Windows Biometric Framework support for their devices as well. According to Belfiore, the company is currently working on designing Windows Hello capable devices, which will ship with the Windows 10 OS.

Ending Note

With the new additions to security features in the Windows 10 OS, Microsoft is clearly looking to make the desktop ecosystem resemble that of a smartphone, which is good news for those who are concerned with security

issues on the new Windows 10 operating system.

Choosing the Best Antivirus for Glitch Free Functioning in Windows 10

An antivirus is the last line of defense against any malware and as you know, the internet is the main source of introducing any harmful element in the system. In case of this new upgrade to windows 10 user has only one option available for selecting a brand an that is Norton. With quality product they also provide satisfactory customers care service. So that user can contact them at the time of any antivirus issue.

This specific brand has released several versions of products which is even compatible with Windows 10's new "Edge" browser. Also, depending upon price user has the liberty to select any version according to their requirements. But before making any purchase you can research online on the Norton's official web forum on certain questions like-

1) Which version should be selected that will run smoothly on windows 10 according to system specs?

2) Is the specific version is compatible with the new Edge browser?

3) Is there need to upgrade the specific antivirus or not?

4) Check whether it is reliable according to existing users.

All these questions are answered by official Norton tech support, they are experienced in dealing with any question of the customer. They are specialized in dealing with issues like antivirus not being able to scan, not responding, under updated software and many more. They usually provide both online and offline services so that users can contact them any time if any one of the source is not available.

However, most users opt to go for toll free number to get a more interactive experience and better applicable solution. This line open full time round the clock so that the user has full freedom to call them any time of day or night.

But if the person is still not satisfied with the answer received from the official sources, it is advised to contact third party tech support companies who are available

24*7 to serve their customers in any technicality. To contact them, visit their official website and give a call on the toll free number mentioned on the website.

Will Windows 10 and Your Printer Play Nice?

Be it an inkjet or an all-in-one printer, the devices have come to be an important part of both homes and offices alike. While the cost of maintenance along with the speed and functionality are just some things to look out for, this article is instead going to talk about compatibility. With Microsoft all set to roll out its Windows 10 OS, making sure your printer is compatible to the new operating system is important for obvious reasons. One of them being, having to look for the drivers that are needed to work the printers.

For those who are running Windows 7 or 8.1 on their PCs, you must have received the invitation for the Windows 10 upgrade by now. And while there are no complaints with those who have worked on Windows 10, considered amongst some of the latest technologies in computer, making sure your peripherals will be compatible with the new Windows 10 is a good idea before you take the leap. The good news here is that Windows 10 drivers are already available for those printers that were built in the past few years. However, the degree of compatibility varies from device to device and model to model. While in some cases, the driver and the software suite could be used with the new OS, on the flip side, compatibility could be limited to just a few particular utilities.

Normally, with major Windows upgrades, there is a good chance that the printer will not be supported, which means users have to forego the upgrade, or get a new printer. To make sure that doesn't happen, here you will find some information on Windows 10 compatibility for certain printers.

Epson

According to Epson, the Windows 10 printer drivers along with the software will be compatible with the Windows 10. Those who own Epson printers can download the driver/utility combo package from the Epson's 'Windows 10 Support page' on the company website. The company states that Windows 10 supports its entire product line, which is good news for the owners of Epson printers.

Hewlett Packard

HP has always been vigilant in keeping its printer compatible with the latest technologies in computer. According to a spokesperson from Hewlett Packard, the company has made sure that all of its printers are compatible with the new Windows 10 operating system. HP has invested heavily to make sure that all of its printers that are currently in use on the Windows 7 and 8.1 operating system will be compatible with the Windows 10 upgrade also, without the need to install any new drivers. That being said, if problems to arise, HP has advised its users to install the latest driver for Windows 10 instead. HP's LaserJet printers that are currently rolling out of the manufacturing belt will come with Windows 10 compatibility right out of the box.

Dell

Another popular brand for printers is Dell. The company has released a list of compatible printer models on its website, which will be supporting the new Windows 10 upgrade. Dell has gone a step further in making it easy for its customers by providing information on whether the drivers are going to be available via a CD that comes along the printer, downloadable from its website or available with the Windows 10 upgrade. So, finding the fix shouldn't take too long.

Canon

Canon is one of the top selling printer brands in the US, and a quick look on its website will give you all the information you need of whether or not your Canon printer is compatible with Windows 10 or not. From what we could gather, most Canon printers are, but to make sure you can always click on the particular model and its category to get information on the drivers.

Panasonic

Panasonic does not seem to be supporting the new Windows 10 upgrade at the moment. But, according to reports, the company will provide support for the OS in a few months time.

Other printers such as XYZ printing's da Vinci 3D printer, Xerox's Version 3 and 4, and printers from MakerBot, Brother, Aleph Objects and OKI Data Americas will all seamlessly integrate with the new Windows 10 OS.

How to Gain Space in the Taskbar of Windows 10 Hiding Options that do Not Use

Having taken a back seat in Windows 8, the taskbar has become a protagonist in Windows 10. This bar is now always visible, even if we are working in tablet mode, and the new system options, as Cortana and Vista, which had their own shortcuts inside the bar.

Even so, there are users who do not like these shortcuts present there as they spend space that could be used to display more applications. The same goes for certain options of the system tray, such as Notification Center, or the touchpad buttons changer and language. Would it not be nice to have the option to hide them when you do not need?

Fortunately, it is possible to hide these icons from the bar relatively easily. Here is how:

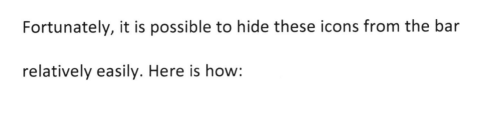

The icon / bar Cortana can be hidden by right-clicking the taskbar> select the menu Cortana> click Hide.

The task view button is hidden by right-clicking the taskbar and then unchecking the Show task view button.

Same for the touch pad button, but unchecking the Show touchpad button.

To hide the other you have to dive more system options.

Right click on the taskbar, and then click Properties.

In the window that appears, click on "Customize" (button next to "Notification Area").

Hide Icons in Windows 10

Here we have two new options to hide icons of the taskbar. The first is to click the link above Select the icons that appear in the taskbar. From there you can hide application icons (such as onedrive, Spotify, and the like).

The other option is available on the link Turn system icons on or off Clicking there we can hide icons such as Notification Center and keyboard language selector (and if we are radicals, we can literally hide all the icons on the toolbar).

As a further step, we can get open applications are displayed in small buttons on the taskbar, without the text that is normally displayed next to them. To achieve this, we must return to the window Properties of the Taskbar and Start Menu and select the option Always combine and hide tabs, located in the " taskbar buttons " section.

"I hid all the icons; now how do I access the system settings?"

Someone may say " of course, we won a lot of space, but now I cannot access Cortana, the task view, or

Notification Center ". Fortunately, Windows 10 has shortcuts to invoke these options without using the task bar. Shortcuts are as follows:

Cortana: can be invoked with WIN + Q keys (for entering text) or WIN + C (to enter voice commands). You can also search by pressing the Windows key and starting to write.

Tasks view: WIN + TAB.

Notification Center: WIN + A.

Changing keyboard language: WIN + Space key.

Additionally, if we are to work with many apps on the taskbar may serve the shortcut key number + WIN , WIN + 1 where the first application opens anchored in the bar, WIN + 2 opens the second, and so on.

Windows 10 is not just an update like those that arrive every few years.

If it is compared with Windows 8, it is a classic for the user, but in many other ways revolutionary operating system. It is the first of a new model that Microsoft called "Windows as a service ', in which the operating system is no longer a product. It is a kind of environment that is updated all the time and meets the needs of the ecosystem: more or less the same happens today with mobile platforms.

It also marks a before and after in the way that Microsoft understands the consumer technology. Until Windows 8, a new version of the operating system had the great goal of selling more computers. Today, that is no longer a

priority: there will be a consistent supply of new
equipment until the end of the year.

MICROSOFT WANTS WINDOWS TO BE THE GATEWAY

Windows is the gateway to Bing, OneNote, Office, Xbox,
Skype and others.

I tested the successive versions of Windows 10
assessment I use a UX32B Asus Intel Core i7 2.4 GHz with
10 GB of RAM. I chose a powerful computer so that
performance is not a problem for the experience, and that
the operating system could offer its best without
bottlenecks. The PC was formatted and had clean
installation of W10.

I must make an advance warning: -and all operating systems technology products in general tend to decrease performance as the months pass, and this evaluation cannot take that into account. The true quality of Windows 10 can only be confirmed if it remains agile and reliable after a year or two of continuous use, which should improve the platform as a service model, with quick fixes and agile improvements.

How to Uninstall and Re-install Windows 10 Built-in Apps

Windows 10 is shipped with many elegant, built-in universal apps that have been developed to help users get maximum experience from the operating system. Some of the built-in universal apps such as Microsoft Edge, Cortana, Xbox, Windows Hello, Music and Windows Store makes this intelligent operating system a perfect fit for both desktop and mobile users.

However, this doesn't mean that all the apps may be useful. Apart from occupying the additional memory space on your computer, some of the apps may slow down the operation of your computer—especially if your computer has a low processing power.

Uninstalling these apps may not be easy. I know you're now asking, "Why can't I just use the normal way of using the Control Panel?" In this chapter, we subdivide the process of dealing with adding and removing Windows 10 integrated apps in four categories. These categories are:

Removing a particular built-in app

Removing all the built-in apps

Reinstalling specific built-in app

Reinstalling all the built-in apps

For you to remove Windows 10 integrated apps, you'll be required to use PowerShell. Let's start by discussing what a Windows PowerShell is.

A Windows PowerShell is a task automation tool that has been included in the operating system to help advanced users—like you—perform system administration tasks. It has been developed using the.NET framework and uses a command-line shell together with its associated scripting language to help System Administrators perform advanced functions.

One such task that a PowerShell can help you with is the process of uninstalling and re-installing Windows 10 universal apps. For you to start Windows PowerShell, perform the following procedures:

On the Start menu, locate the search button and type: "PowerShell."

Once the PowerShell has been found in the search results, right-click on it and choose "Run as Administrator.

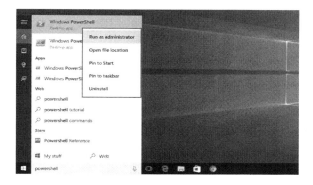

A Windows PowerShell command prompt appears as

shown below.

You'll be expected to use a scripting language to help you

uninstall and re-install Windows 10 built-in apps. For

instance, the syntax for removing apps is:

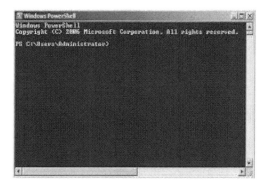

"Remove-AppxPackage" where "AppxPackage" is the

application that you'd like to uninstall. So, if you want to

remove an application, then you have to type: "Remove-

AppxPackage" at the command prompt.

So, without further ado, let's jump in and find out how you can remove and re-install some of the common Windows 10 universal apps.

#1: Removing a specific built-in app

For you to uninstall an app in Windows 10, it's important to get all the information about that application. For instance, you may want to get all the information about all the apps that have been installed on your system.

The scripting language syntax for getting all the information about all apps in your system is: "Get-AppxPackage" which is typed at the command prompt. This command will display all the apps that have been installed on your computer. You can now find out the specific details of an app that you want to remove from your system.

Here are steps that you can follow if you wish to uninstall a particular built-in app in Windows 10:

Open your Windows PowerShell. On the start menu, type: "PowerShell" in the search button. From the results that appear, right click on the PowerShell and select "Run as an Administrator."

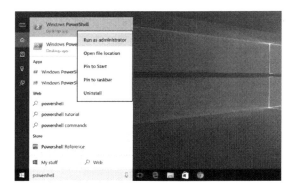

In the PowerShell command prompt window that appears type "Get-AppxPackage |Remove-AppxPackage."

Press the Enter key and wait for the app to be uninstalled from your computer.

So, how can you get started?

Well, in the examples below, we explain how you can uninstall specific programs from your computer. If you want to remove a specific program, just copy and paste one or more of the following commands in the Windows PowerShell command prompt. Once you've copied and pasted in your Windows PowerShell command prompt, ensure you press the enter key.

Here's a quick way to see the process in action:

Removing the Alarms and Clock

Type or Copy/Paste: "Get-AppxPackage *windowsalarms* | Remove-AppxPackage" at the Windows PowerShell command prompt.

Press the enter key and hold on for the uninstallation process to be completed.

Removing 3D Builder

Type or copy/paste: "Get-AppxPackage *3dbuilder* | Remove-AppxPackage" at the command prompt.

Press the enter key and hold on for the uninstallation process to be completed.

Removing the Camera

Type or copy/paste: "Get-AppxPackage *windowscamera* | Remove-AppxPackage" at the Windows PowerShell command prompt.

Press the enter key and hold on for the uninstallation process to be completed.

Removing the Calculator App

Type or copy/paste: "Get-AppxPackage

windowscalculator | Remove-AppxPackage" at the

Windows PowerShell command prompt.

Press the enter key and hold on for the uninstallation

process to be completed.

Removing Get Office App

Type or copy/paste: "Get-AppxPackage *officehub* |

Remove-AppxPackage" at the Windows PowerShell

command prompt.

Press the enter key and hold on for the uninstallation

process to be completed.

Removing the Get Skype App

Type or copy/paste: "Get-AppxPackage *skypeapp* |
Remove-AppxPackage" at the Windows PowerShell
command prompt.

Press the enter key and hold on for the uninstallation
process to be completed.

Uninstall Get Started App

Type or copy/paste: "Get-AppxPackage *getstarted* |
Remove-AppxPackage" at the Windows PowerShell
command prompt.

Press the enter key and hold on for the uninstallation
process to be completed.

Removing Maps

Type or copy/paste: "Get-AppxPackage *windowsmaps* |

Remove-AppxPackage" at the Windows PowerShell

command prompt.

Press the enter key and hold on for the uninstallation

process to be completed.

Uninstalling Microsoft Solitaire Collection App

Type or copy/paste: "Get-AppxPackage

solitairecollection | Remove-AppxPackage" at the

Windows PowerShell command prompt.

Press the enter key and hold on for the uninstallation

process to be completed.

Uninstalling People App

Type or copy/paste: "Get-AppxPackage *people* |

Remove-AppxPackage" at the Windows PowerShell

command prompt.

Press the enter key and hold on for the uninstallation

process to be completed.

Uninstalling the Xbox App

Type or copy/paste: "Get-AppxPackage *xboxapp* |

Remove-AppxPackage" at the Windows PowerShell

command prompt.

Press the enter key and hold on for the uninstallation

process to be completed.

That's it. We haven't exhausted all the Windows 10

universal apps. Now that we've explained the process

using 11 apps, you should now be in a position to uninstall

any built-in app in Windows 10. The process is simple and

straightforward. Just remember—type: "Get-AppxPackage |Remove-AppxPackage" at the Windows PowerShell command prompt, press the Enter key and hold on the uninstallation process to be completed.

#2: Removing all the built-in apps

If you'd like to ensure that your Windows 10 doesn't have any built-in apps, then you have to remove all provisioned apps. The good thing is that you can achieve this with one single command. Wondering how this is possible?

Well, for you to uninstall all the app, follow the following steps:

Open the Windows PowerShell as an Administrator by opening the start menu and typing "PowerShell" on the search button.

Once the PowerShell has been located in the search

results, right-click on it and select "Run as Administrator.

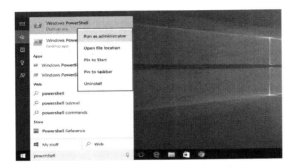

Type "Get-AppxPackage | Remove-AppxPackage" at the

Windows PowerShell command prompt and press the

enter key and hold on until all the built-in apps have been

removed.

Now, the above command can only remove the programs

for the current user account. In some instances, you may

want to remove all the apps for all user accounts. For you

to remove all the apps for all users in the system, follow

the following steps:

Open the Windows PowerShell as an Administrator by opening the start menu and typing "PowerShell" on the search button.

Once the PowerShell has been located in the search results, right-click on it and select "Run as Administrator.

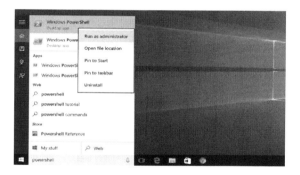

Now, type "Get-AppxPackage -allusers | Remove-AppxPackage" at the command prompt and press enter key. Hold on for the uninstallation process to complete.

It's not advisable to remove all the universal, built-in apps in Windows 10. This is because you may affect the normal operation of your computer.

#3: Reinstalling specific built-in app

The fact that you removed a particular Windows 10 integrated app should not cause you unnecessary stress is you want to re-install that app. Here's what you should do in case you'd like to restore a particular built-in app in Windows 10:

Open the Windows PowerShell as an Administrator by opening the start menu and typing "PowerShell" on the search button.

Once the PowerShell has been located in the search results, right-click on it and select "Run as Administrator.

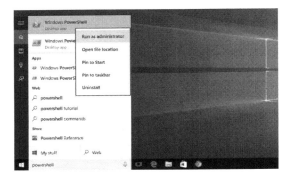

Now, type or copy/paste this text at the Windows PowerShell: "Add-AppxPackage -register appxmanifest.xml_file_path —DisableDevelopmentMode". Re-installing a specific app requires you to specify the full path to the "appxmanifest.xml" file that's located in "C:\Program Files\WindowsApps" folder.

For instance, to re-install Xbox on your system, type or copy/paste "Add-AppxPackage *xboxapp* -register "C:\Program Files\WindowsApps\PackageFullName\appxmanifest.xml" —DisableDevelopmentMode

Hold on for the re-installation process to be completed.

#4: Reinstalling all the built-in apps

A single command can remove all the built-in apps in Windows 10. Here's a quick way to see the process in action:

Open the Windows PowerShell as an Administrator by opening the start menu and typing "PowerShell" on the search button.

Once the PowerShell has been located in the search results, right-click on it and select "Run as Administrator.

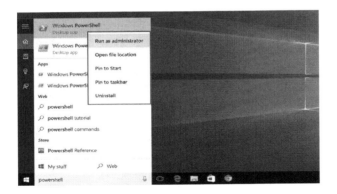

Now, type or copy/paste "Get-AppxPackage -allusers | foreach {Add-AppxPackage -register

"$($_.InstallLocation)\appxmanifest.xml" -

DisableDevelopmentMode}" at the Windows PowerShell

command prompt and press the enter key.

Wait for the re-installation process to be completed.

Restart your computer so that the changes takes effect.

Now that we've explained the process of installing and

uninstalling Windows 10 apps, you should be in a position

to install and remove any built-in app in Windows 10.

Fixing Display and Sound issues in Windows 10

If you've used Windows 10 for a while and you realize that some programs don't display their fonts properly, then you're not alone. You may have attempted to check your screen resolution to ensure that it is correctly set. Most users have complained about this problem too. This phenomenon has been referred to as **blurry font** problem in Windows 10.

It's a problem that all Windows 10 users who have upgraded from previous versions have encountered especially with applications such as iTunes and Internet Explorer 9.

I know you're now thinking, "What are blurry fonts?"

Well, blurry fonts, as the name suggests, are fonts that appear fuzzy, unclear and lacks proper definition. You may encounter this problem even if your computer has a very high-resolution display screen. If you are faced with this problem, you shouldn't bother trying to change the displays settings on your PC. Because that won't work.

This is because some programs such as ITunes and Internet Explorer 9—that you were previously using in earlier versions of Windows—may not have been properly tailored to use the blurred fonts that Windows 10 is used to. As a matter of fact, Window 10 OS has been developed to use a different Dots per Inch (DPI)—which means that earlier versions of apps may not display their fonts properly in it.

The application that you're using has to be customized to adjust the DPI settings for Windows 10 if the fonts are to be displayed correctly. As a Windows user or administrator, it's upon you to configure these settings so that fonts in these programs can be displayed correctly.

Now, that's not all. Besides the blurry font's problem, you have to ensure that your sound system is working correctly—especially if you've upgraded to Windows 10 from Windows 7 or Windows 8. This is especially true when you're using programs such as Skype or WhatsApp to communicate. The fact is—different vendors manufacture most sound devices, therefore whenever you upgrade to Windows 10, you should also update the driver to ensure it's in sync with your OS.

So, how can get around display and sound issues in Windows 10? Good question.

Let's dive in and find out procedures to fix these problems.

#1: Fixing Blurry Fonts

As I had mentioned earlier, the issue of blurry fonts can't be resolved by adjusting the screen resolution. For you to fix this issue, you can fix the blurry font for the specific program that's having the font issue problem. Or, you can use a third-party program to help you.

Let's find out how these two approaches work in resolving the blurry fonts problem.

#1: Fixing Blurry Fonts for a specific program

For you to fix the blurry font for a particular application, follow the steps outlined below:

Locate the app that's having the blurry font problem.

Once you locate the app, right-click on it. For instance, if it's iTunes that's is having the blurry fonts problem, and then you should find its shortcut on the Desktop of your PC and right-click on it.

Now, from the context menu that appears, click on the

"**Properties**" tab.

You should now see a window similar to one displayed above. Click on the "**Compatibility**" tab.

Under the "**Settings**" section of the window, click on the

"*Disable display scaling on high DPI settings*" checkbox.

Don't forget to click on the "**Apply**" button so that your

changes can be saved.

#2: Using a third party program

You can also download and install a third-party software

to help you fix the blurry fonts issue in Windows 10. Of

course, there are some programs that you can use. An

example of such a software is the XPExplorer—which is a

popular open source program that you can easily

download and correct the blurry font problem.

Here are steps that explain how you can use the

XPExplorer to fix the Windows 10 blurry fonts problem:

Download and install the program on your computer. You

can use search engines to locate the program.

Once you've installed the application, ensure you reboot

your computer so that your changes can be effected.

Now, open the program.

Select the "*Use Windows 8.1 DPI Scaling*" option for all

your programs.

Don't forget to click on the "*Apply*" button for the

changes to be effected.

Fixing the sound problem in Windows 10

The sound problem can be fixed by checking whether the

driver for the sound device has been installed and is

updated. If the sound driver is missing, then you'll have to

download it and install it. However, if you find that the

driver is installed, and you're still having sound problem,

then you should try configuring the sound devices.

Here are steps that can help you resolve such problems:

Right-click on the sound icon on the taskbar. The sound

icon is usually placed on the taskbar at the bottom right

end of your desktop. From the context menu, that's

displayed, click on "**Playback Devices**."

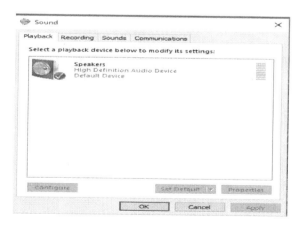

Now, chose the playback device that you are currently using—this will be speakers in most cases. Double-click on the Speakers so that you display its properties as shown the screenshot below:

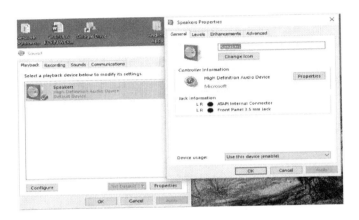

Locate the "Advanced" tab of the window that appears and click on it. Try adjusting the bit rate for your device to either 24bit/44100 Hz or 24bit/192000Hz. This will depend on the device that you are using.

Alternatively, you can uninstall the current sound driver and re-instal it. But make sure you update the driver after

the installation process. Here are steps that can help you
to uninstall and re-install the sound driver on your PC:

On the start menu, type "Device Manager" on the search
button and press the enter key.

Right-click on the Device Manager and select "*Run as*
Administrator."

Locate your sound and audio devices from the window
that's displayed.

Right-click on your current sound driver that has been
installed. Right-click on it and select "Uninstall".

Reboot your PC so that changes can be effected.

Once you reboot, start the Device Manager and locate the sound and audio devices.

Right-click on your current sound driver that has been installed. Right-click on it and select "Scan for Hardware Changes".

Wait for the update process to take effect. You should be connected to a high-speed internet connection.

Reboot your PC for the changes to be effected.

And there you have it—you should be able to resolve blurry fonts and sound problems in Windows 10.

Drivers and Software Compatibility issues in Windows 10

It's no secret that the process of fixing drivers and software compatibility problems can be tedious and time-consuming. In fact, the process can turn into a nightmare if you've just upgraded from either Windows 7 or Windows 8.

It's important to note that all the versions of Windows OS—Windows 10 included—have some generic drivers which are shipped with the OS. However, most of the drivers are developed by third party companies. So, if you've just upgraded to Windows 10 from Windows 7 or Windows 8—where you were using third party drivers—you may find that some drivers are not compatible with Windows 10.

As a Windows 10 user or administrator, it's important to learn how to fix such errors. The same applies to software compatibility. Fact is— most programs that were developed for earlier versions of Windows OS—such as WinXP, Win 7 or even Win 8—still works in Windows 10. But not all of these apps may be compatible with Windows 10.

If an app isn't compatible with Windows 10, you should be in a position to troubleshoot and rectify the errors. In this chapter, we explain techniques that can help you fix both driver and software compatibility issues.

Are you ready? Let's dive in.

Fixing Drivers issues in Windows 10

If there's one expectation that Windows 10 has surpassed concerning improving user experience, then it is its ability to bundle most of the drivers—including those from third-party developers—into one system. So, whether you have a printer, keyboard or a network interface card, you'll always find your driver shipped with Windows 10.

But that may not be the case always. Not all the drivers for hardware devices—especially those from third party developers—may integrate well with Windows 10. Most users that have upgraded their OS's from either Windows 7 or Windows 8 have complained of driver compatibility problems that arises from upgrading to Windows 10.

If you're confronted with this issue, there are two methods that can help you fix the driver compatibility problems. You can either update your driver or install it manually. Let's find out.

#1: Updating the driver

If you've upgraded to Windows 10 and you find that one driver that was working correctly in your previous OS isn't working properly, then you need to update that driver. To upgrade the driver that has already been installed on your PC, follow the steps below:

On the start menu, click on "**Settings**."

Once the settings menu has been displayed, click on "**Devices**" and the select "**Device Manager**."

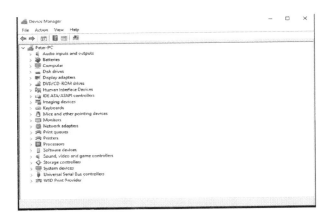

Locate the device whose driver isn't working properly. For instance, if the graphics card isn't working correctly, then select it under the "Display Adapters." Right-click on the

adapters name to show the name of the adapter that

should be updated.

From the context menu, that's displayed, click on "**Update**

Driver Software."

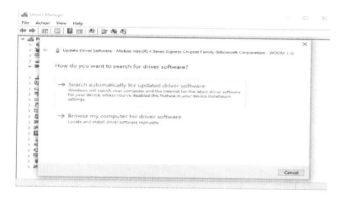

Now, choose the "**Search automatically for updated**

driver software" option from the window that appears.

Hold on for the search process to be completed. The

wizard will search for the available updates of the driver

on the internet. So, ensure you're connected to the

internet. Follow the on-screen instructions to complete

the update process of your driver.

#2: Installing Drivers Manually

If you've just installed your fresh copy of Windows 10, and

you find that one driver is missing, then you can download

it and install it manually. You can check if the driver is

installed or not by following the steps below:

On the start menu, click on "*Settings*."

Once the settings menu has been displayed, click on

"*Devices*" and the select "*Device Manager*."

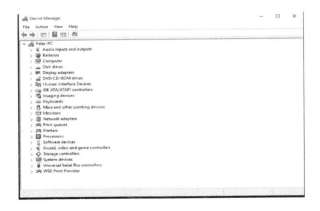

If the driver for a particular device is missing, there will be a question mark displayed against the device name. In my case, all the drivers have been installed—that's why there's no question mark displayed against any of the devices.

If you find that one driver is missing, then here are steps that can help you to download and install that driver on your computer:

Download the driver for the device that you want to be installed on your computer. Ensure you select the right operating system for your driver—in this case is Windows 10. Apart from selecting the right OS, ensure you've chosen the correct number of bits for your OS. If your OS is a 32-bit, then ensure that driver you download is compatible with 32-bit Windows 10.

If your driver is a ".msi" or a ".exe" file, then double-click

on it to initialize the installation process. For instance, the

screen below shows how a Realtek card reader driver can

be installed on a Windows 10 PC.

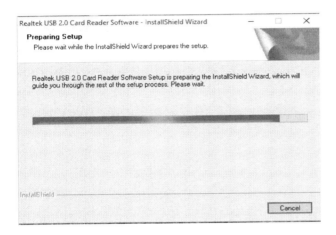

Follow the on-screen instructions to finish the installation

process. Restart your PC so that the changes can be

effected.

What if the driver you've downloaded isn't a ".msi" or a

".exe"?

If your driver isn't a ".msi" or a ".exe", then here are steps

that you should follow to install it on your Windows 10

PC:

Extract the driver file that you've just downloaded to a

folder that you can easily find on your PC.

On the start menu, click on "*Settings*."

From the settings menu, select "*Devices*" and click on

"*Device Manager*."

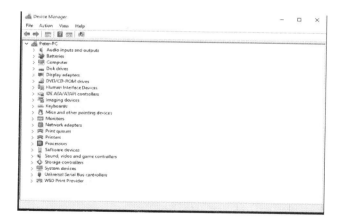

Now, select the device whose driver is missing. For

instance, if wish to install the Graphic card's driver, then select the "*Display Adapters*" and right-click on the

adapters name.

Once the content menu has been displayed, click on

"*Update Driver Software*."

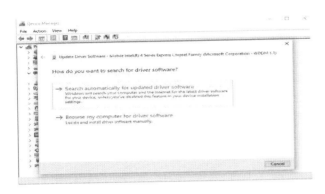

From the window that appears, select "Browse my

computer for driver software."

Now, click on the "Browse" button so that you locate the

folder where the driver files were extracted. Make sure

you tick the "Include subfolders" checkbox for the wizard

to search automatically for the appropriate driver in all

the sub-folders.

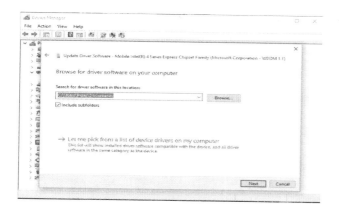

Click on the "Next" button so that the wizard searches a suitable driver in the folder and sub-folders where driver files were extracted.

Once the driver file has been found, follow the on-screen instructions so that the driver can be installed on your computer

Make sure you restart your PC.

Fixing Software Compatibility issues in Windows 10

The problem of program compatibility arises when you upgrade your OS to Windows 10. Or, if you've installed a fresh copy of Windows 10 and you wish to install an app that was developed using old technologies that are not compatible with Windows 10.

Software compatibility issues can be handled by either a Program Compatibility Troubleshooter or you can change the compatibility settings for the program that's not working correctly in Windows 10. Let's jump in and find out how you can fix these problems on your Windows 10 system.

#1: How to run a Program Compatibility Troubleshooter

To run a Program Compatibility Troubleshooter, follows the steps below:

On the start menu, look for the search button and type "run programs" in it.

From the results that are displayed, click on "**Run programs made for previous versions of Windows.**"

Click the "**Next**" button to launch the Program Compatibility Troubleshooter.

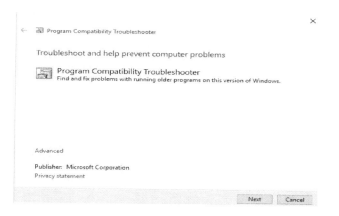

A list of programs that are not compatible with Windows 10 will be displayed. Select the program that you wish to fix. In case the application isn't listed, click on "**Not listed**" and follow the on-screen instruction to locate the app that you want to troubleshoot.

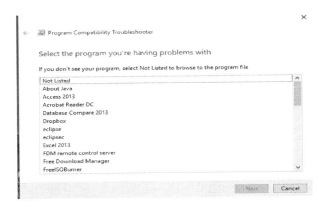

Once you've selected the right application, click on the "Next" button.

Follow the on-screen instructions of the wizard to resolve the program compatibility issue.

#2: How to change the compatibility settings manually

To change the compatibility settings for an application manually, follow the steps outlined below:

On the start menu, look for the search button and type the name of the program that you'd like to troubleshoot.

In the search results that appear, right-click on the name

of the software that you'd like to troubleshoot and click

on "**Open file location**." For instance, to troubleshoot

VLC, right-click on it and select "*Open file location*"

Right-click on the name of your software and click on

"**Properties.**"

From the context menu that appears, click on

"**Compatibility.**"

Now, choose one or more of the settings—depending on how you'd like the problem to be resolved. The table below provides an explanation of the different settings.

Setting	Description
Compatibility mode	Use this option if you know that your program works well in the OS that you have selected.
Reduced color mode	Use this option if you want your program to use very limited colors of your computer system.

Run in 640 × 480 screen resolution	Use this option if you know that your graphics have been rendered incorrectly.
Disable display scaling on high DPI settings	Use this option if you want to display your fonts correctly.
Change settings for all users	Use this option if you want to apply the compatibility settings for all users on your computer.

Once you've selected the appropriate settings, click on the "OK" button to complete the set-up process.

There you have it! Can you now troubleshoot any driver or software compatibility on your computer without hassles?

Tweaking the performance of Windows 10

There's no doubt about improved experiences that Windows has provided to their users compared to its predecessors. Let's face it—Windows 10 has continued to provide greater user experiences that's is unrivaled when matched with either Windows 7 or Windows 8. And make no mistake—Windows 10 will continue to shape how desktop computers operate and even mobile devices, now and in future.

However, the fact that this intelligent OS has improved user experience regarding enhanced performance doesn't mean that it is perfect. Truth be told—you have to tweak its performance for you realize the greater experiences that come with this intuitively integrated touchscreen and desktop OS.

In fact, improving the performance of your Windows 10 will ensure that you're operating optimally. This means that you'll be utilizing the limited memory capacities of your computer at optimal speed. So, if you're convinced that your Windows 10 performance should be tweaked, then let's jump in and learn four methods that can help you.

#1: Minimize the paging file

Of course, the first thing that you should do is to make sure the paging file has been minimized. I'm sure you're now asking, "What is a paging file?"

Well, a paging file is a file that's used by an OS to support system crash dumps. Besides supporting system crash dumps, it also allows your computer system to use the physical RAM more efficiently. If you have a PC with less

RAM capacity—less than 8GB—then minimizing the paging file is a MUST if you'd like to have improved performances.

On the other hand, if your computer has a memory that's larger than 8GB, then Windows 10 can be easily the paging file automatically—so you won't be required to configure it manually. For you to minimize the paging file for your computer, follow the steps outlined below:

Right-click on your start menu and click on the *"**System**."* You should see a screenshot similar to the one below.

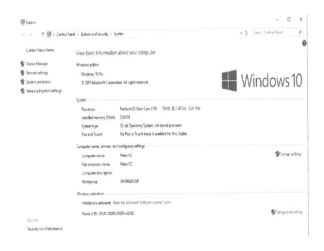

Click on the "***Advanced system settings***" tab and click the

"***Settings***" button that appears in the **Performance**

section.

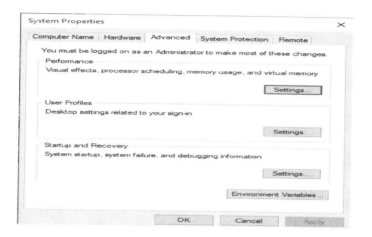

Locate the Performance Options dialog box and click on

"***Change***" button. The change button appears in the

Advanced Tab under the Virtual Memory section. You

should see a screenshot similar to the one below.

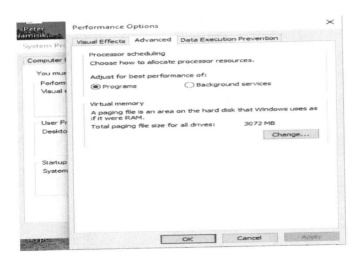

While in the Virtual Memory dialog box, scroll down to
the "*Minimum Allowed*", the "*Recommended*" and the
"*Currently Allocated Paging File Sizes*."

Now, click to uncheck the "*Automatically manage paging
file size for all drives*" check box. You should see a
screenshot similar to the one below.

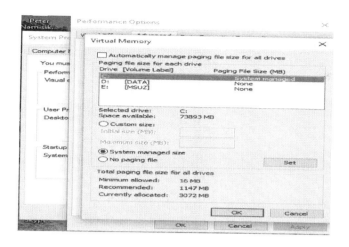

Select the "**Custom Size**", and then type the values into

the Initial Size (MB) and the Maximum Size (MB) boxes.

The typed values should range from IGB to 4GB

depending on the size of your RAM.

Click on the "**Set**" and the "**OK**." Buttons respectively.

Don't forget to reboot your computer so that changes can

be saved.

#2: Disable Visual Effects

Another way of improving performance in Windows 10 is disabling the visual effects. Despite the fact that animations and shadows make an excellent and intuitive user interface, they also use a lot of CPU and RAM capacities. Disabling these effects can significantly improve the performance of your system. Here are steps that can help you disable the visual effects in Windows 10:

Right-click on the start menu and click on the "**System**." You should now see a screenshot similar to the one shown below.

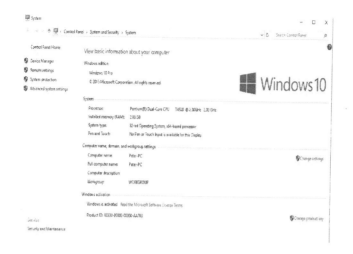

Click on the Advanced system settings tab and select the

"*Visual Effects*" button that appears in the Performance

section. The screenshot below shows what you should

see.

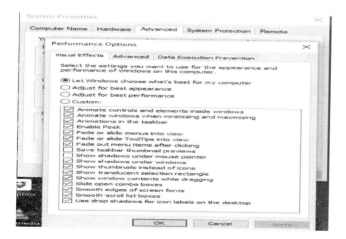

Make sure you "Uncheck" all the options that have been displayed as "Checked" so that they are disabled.

Click on the "**Apply**" button and "**OK**" respectively to apply the changes.

#3: Minimize Startup programs

The number of startup programs can significantly degraded the performance of your PC. You should strive to have minimum number of startup apps if you want to have improved performance with Windows 10. Here are steps that can help you minimize the number of startup programs in Windows 10:

Open the task manager. You can press Ctrl + Alt + Del or right-click on the task bar and select "Task Manager."

From the window that appears, click on the startup tab.

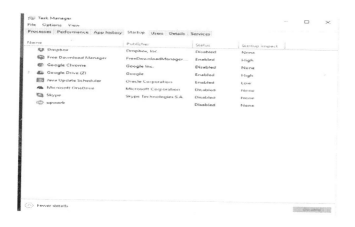

Disable the unnecessary programs that you think are slowing down your PC.

Reboot your computer so that changes can be saved.

#4: Disable unnecessary services

When you boot Windows 10, there may be a couple of unnecessary services that run in the background. These services may not be essential for you. You can disable these services if you want to tweak the performance of your system.

Here are steps that can help you disable the unnecessary services in Windows 10:

Right-click on *"**This PC**"* icon which is placed on the Desktop.

Click on *"**Manage.**"*

Click on the *"**Services and Applications**"* that appears in the left pane of the window.

Select *"**Services.**"*

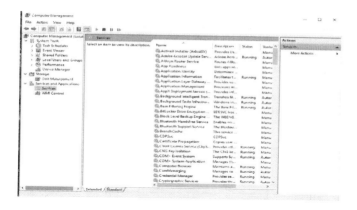

Right-click on the service that you want to disable and the

click "*stop*."

That's it.

How to Secure Windows 10 Systems

By now, you should have realized that Windows 10 is both a desktop and a cloud operating system. When the cloud functionality is added to Windows 10, it means security issues will also increase multifold. This is because you'll be sharing your data far more with Microsoft and all its partner clients than ever before.

For instance, Windows 10 OS periodically collects the keystrokes and even the voice to help it improve spell-checking and voice recognition. This is despite it not having a key logger as previous OS's had. It's important to know that all cloud-based services collect data from users without the knowledge of users. For instance, Google Docs, the Siri, the Office 365 all collect information even if your OS is lacking a keystroke logger.

But this doesn't mean that you should panic when using Windows 10. Truth be told—Windows 10 is the most secure Windows OS ever. It has more built-in security protections that can help to safeguard you against malware, viruses, phishing than any other version of Windows. For instance, new features can now be delivered through automatic updates as opposed to earlier versions of Windows.

So, what are some of the features that Microsoft has introduced in Windows 10 to help you manage security-related problems? Let's find out.

Windows 10 Built-in Security Protections

Here are some of the built-in applications that can help you protect your Windows 10 system:

#1: Windows Hello

I'm very certain that you have more than one password. Having many passwords can be disastrous especially if you're forgetful. Now, Windows 10 has introduced Windows Hello to help you address the challenges of having so many passwords. With the Windows Hello, you'll use a biometrics to help you log into your systems.

So, if you're the type that keeps on forgetting passwords, then Windows Hello can help you manage your system well without having to keep on remembering passwords. You can use your fingerprints, eyes, or even face to help you log into your system.

#2: Microsoft Edge

The first thing that you do when you log in to Windows OS is start up the browser. Well, Windows 10 has developed an all-new browser—Microsoft Edge—that's designed to offer more security than other browsers. Microsoft Edge uses advanced technologies that give browsing a personal touch than other versions of browsers.

#3: SmartScreen

To protect your system from phishing sites while using a Microsoft Edge browser, then you should consider activating the SmartScreen app. This app will help you from malicious users that may want to steal your identity and other personal information details such as credit card details. Ideally, the SmartScreen app defends your PC from socially-engineered downloads that are cloud-based.

#4: Windows Defender

Perhaps Windows Defender is one of the revolutionary built-in apps that you can find in Windows 10. Other previous versions were not shipped with Windows

Defender. It's a robust anti-malware solution that is included in Windows 10 to help you stay protected. If you're worried about which antivirus to install on your Windows 10, then Windows Defender will protect your system.

Besides, it's continuously updated so that it meets the evolving threats as they are identified. Because of this feature, it's always quick to detect and protect your system against any emerging malware.

#5: Family Features

With some a few clicks, Windows 10 can help you keep your family safer while online. The Microsoft family features to keep your kids safer by blocking unwanted content such as adult sites and inappropriate apps and games.

Measures to secure Windows 10 System

Despite the presence of the built-in apps in Windows 10, you still have to take precautions to secure your PC. As I had indicated earlier, Windows 10 is both PC based and cloud-based OS. The fact that it's a cloud-based OS means that security problems will increase exponentially with online risks being reported on a daily basis.

So, how can you protect your Windows 10 from these risks? Let's dive in and find out measures that you can undertake to secure your system.

#1: Firewall Management

Firewalls can be regarded as network security programs that can grant or reject network access to some traffic flows between untrusted zones such as the Internet and other untrusted network areas such as a corporate network.

Windows 10 comes with a pre-installed firewall utility. Although the firewall service is always turned on in Windows 10, you may find out that it's been turned off—especially if you installed some apps. As a matter of fact, some apps require that you disable the firewall utility before they can get installed on a Windows 10. One such application is Microsoft SQL Server.

In such instances, you should ensure that your firewall is turned. In fact, your firewall should always be on to help block traffic that may come from untrusted network zones.

To turn on the firewall, follow the steps below:

Click the start menu, type "**Control Panel**" on the search button and press the enter key.

Locate "**System and Security**" menu from the items that are listed in the Control Panel.

Click on the "**Windows Firewall**."

If the Firewall is disabled, then its Windows Firewall state should be "Off." To turn it on, navigate to left pane and click "Turn Windows Firewall On or off."

In the window that appears, click "Turn on Windows Firewall" and the OK button.

To turn off the firewall, follow the steps below:

Click the start menu, type "**Control Panel**" on the search button and press the enter key.

Locate "*System and Security*" menu from the items that are listed in the Control Panel.

Click on the "*Windows Firewall*."

If the Firewall is enabled, then its Windows Firewall state should be "On." To turn it off, navigate to left pane and click "Turn Windows Firewall On or off."

In the window that appears, click "Turn off Windows Firewall" and the OK button.

It's not recommended to turn off your firewall. You should only turn off your firewall if you're troubleshooting a problem or installing another firewall.

#2: Management of passwords and policies

Even though passwords are being replaced by biometrics, one-time password tokens, and smart cards, they continue to provide a popular approach for most users when it comes to logging into systems. Make no mistake—the use of passwords is going remain popular for a very long time to come. Of course, several reasons have made the use of passwords to be popular among Windows users.

Apart from offering cheaper alternatives to deploy, passwords can be combined with credentials to create stronger authentication systems that provide foolproof security to an organization. But this will only depend on a strong password policy. As a Windows 10 Administrator, it's vital for you to put in place a password policy for an organization.

A strong password policy is important for several reasons. If you think about for some time, you'll realize that your users have a right to access the system resources. Now, these resources should be protected at all costs. A password policy will ensure that malicious users don't take advantage of weaknesses in password systems to gain unauthorized entry into that resource.

You can protect your Windows 10 PC by customizing the password policy settings. These include requiring your users to change their password frequently, limiting the minimum length for the user's passwords and requiring the passwords to meet individual requirements.

If you're convinced that a password policy is required in an organization to promote the security of data resources, then let's jump in to find out how you can set your password policy.

Here are steps that can help you set a password policy for your Windows 10 PC:

Click the Start button and type "*secpol.msc*" into the search button that appears. You need Administrative privileges, or if you're in a domain, then you should be the Network Administrator.

Click on the "*secpol*" so that you open the Local Security Policy. Administrator privilege permission is required. If you're prompted for the administrator password, then type your password or provide your confirmation.

Now, double click on "Account Policies" that appears in the left pane of your window and click the "*Password Policy*."

Double-click an item in the Policy list that you wish to change, and then click "*Change the setting*."

Click "*OK*" button to save the changes.

#3: Hard Drive Encryption

It's often said that information is power. So, if your PC is stolen, then it would mean that you'll have no access to your information—which is the only power you have. Besides, such data can be taken advantage of or can even be destroyed.

So, how can you protect your information on a hard drive?

One method that has been proposed to deal with protection of data on hard drives is locking the PC with a password. But just locking a PC with a password isn't enough. Today, there exists numerous apps that can unlock your PC in a matter of seconds. In Windows 10, you can use Windows Hello—which relies on biometrics—

to protect your system. But this may not work if the secondary storage device is taken away from the PC.

Only one option is left for you: the BitLocker. The BitLocker can help you secure both your internal and external hard disks. Furthermore, it can also contribute to determining security threats are present during the booting up process. How can you use the BitLocker to secure your hard drive?

Well, here are procedures that you should follow to secure your data:

On the start menu, type *"BitLocker"* in the search button and hit the enter key.

From the results of the search process, click the *"Manage BitLocker."*

Choose the hard drive that you wish to encrypt and then click on *"Turn on BitLocker."*

Next, select how the unlocking should be conducted. You can either use the password or the smart card option.

Select the location where the recovery key should be kept in case you forget the password.

Select how you want the encryption to be done. You can either choose the entire hard drive or the used hard disk space.

#4: Management of Viruses and Worms

If you usually connect to the Internet or allow other people to use your PC, then there are high chances of viruses and worms spreading to your computer. For you to protect your computer from viruses, then you should install an updated antivirus software.

Fortunately, you can use the Windows Defender that's pre-installed in Windows 10 to help you prevent viruses and worms from interfering with your data. Perhaps the Windows Defender is one of the revolutionary built-in apps that you can find in Windows 10. Remember, other previous versions were not shipped with Windows Defender.

Windows Defender is a robust anti-malware solution that is included in Windows 10 to help you stay protected. Furthermore, it's regularly updated so that it meets the evolving threats as they are identified. Because of this feature, it's always quick to detect and protect your system against any emerging malware.

Besides the Windows Defender, here are other measures that you should undertake to prevent viruses and worms from spreading to your PC:

Ensure you turn on the Firewall. A firewall that's turned on can help to protect your PC by preventing malicious software from gaining access to it.

Ensure you update your Windows Defender. An updated Windows Defender can help you to protect your PC against viruses, worms, spyware and other security threats.

Ensure you've installed an antispyware software. Besides using the Windows Defender, ensure that you've installed an antispyware software to help protect your PC from spyware and other unwanted programs.

Ensure your computer is updated. An updated Windows 10 can fix software bugs that can be exploited by hackers to gain unauthorized entry into your system. Therefore, always ensure that your PC is updated.

Network Administration Features of Windows 10

Much of the attention in Windows 10 has been aimed at the attention of consumers, especially the user interface. For instance, while the Metro interface was removed, other administrative tasks such as Network Administration had to be re-configured.

As a matter of fact, Windows 10 has improved the interface for performing most of the network administration tasks such as configuring WI-FI networks, VPN's and management of work groups. For instance, one of the most significant changes that you should have noted by now is the addition of the Settings app.

The Windows 10 Settings app in has now replaced the PC settings app that was found in Windows 8 and even previous versions of Windows. When you open the Settings app, you'll notice that there's a new "Network & Internet" section that's entirely different from previous versions of Windows OS. What Microsoft had done is that they have divided the wireless and the wired connections in various parts.

You can notice these from the Wi-Fi and the Ethernet settings that you see from the "Network & Internet" of the Settings app. doesn't this improve user experience?

Well, with the subdivisions, you can now share and connect to any wireless network with any of your friends that are using the Wi-Fi Sense. Besides, you can also perform all the wireless networking tasks from the Settings section. In this chapter, we explore how you can connect to WI-FI networks, manage the IP addresses, network printers and work groups.

As you've noted, we've left out the Ethernet section. Of course, when you're using the Ethernet, the process of connecting is pretty clear-cut. Connect your Ethernet cable—RJ 45 connector—into the network port and you're good to go. However, for wireless networks, the process may not be straightforward as the Ethernet.

Without further ado, let's dive and find out how you can perform network administration features in Windows 10.

#1: Management of Wireless LAN's

The process of accessing a wireless network—what's commonly known as WI-FI—begins by configuring your wireless adapter. If your computer has a wireless adapter, then you should ensure that you download and install the appropriate driver for that device. Of course, we know that Windows 10 is shipped with most of the pre-installed drivers—with wireless adapters included.

However, you may find that a particular wireless adapter driver that's pre-installed isn't working properly. Especially when you've just upgraded from either Windows 7 or Windows 8. So, the first thing is to ensure that the wireless adapter driver is updated. If it's not updated, then you should update it immediately.

Now, once you have installed—the latest wireless adapter driver—you should now see the new wireless networks. These networks will appear in the system tray that's located at the extreme right of your task bar.

How to connect to Wi-Fi Networks

Here's is how you can connect to a wireless network:

Click on the Network Icon. The Network icon is located in the System tray on the extreme right of the taskbar.

You'll see available wireless networks. Select the wireless network that you'd like to connect to. Ensure that you select the "Connect Automatically" option if you'll be frequently connecting to that network on regular basis.

Click on "Connect" button.

Enter the password to complete the configuration of the wireless network.

How to forget Wi-Fi Networks

If the password of a particular wireless network that you've been regularly connecting to have been changed, then you should forget that network first before typing its new password. Here's how you can forget a wireless network in Windows 10:

Click on the Network Icon. The Network icon is located in the System tray on the extreme right of the taskbar.

You'll see available wireless networks.

Now from the Wi-Fi, click on the "Manage Wi-Fi settings."

You'll see a list of networks that you've been connecting to on a regular basis.

From the list of your wireless networks, click on the relevant network that you wish to forget and then click the "Forget" button to forget the password for that network.

How to access passwords for Wi-Fi networks

If you ever wanted to access and view the passwords for your Wi-Fi network on Windows 7, all you were required was to click the Wi-Fi icon in the system tray. Once you were in the pop-up menu, you'd right-click on the network that you wanted to view the password and get to its properties. Now, inside the properties window, there was a Security tab where you see the Wi-Fi password for that network.

Well, with Windows 10, it has become a bit difficult. You can't use the same approach you used in Windows 7. Here's how you can access the passwords for Wi-Fi networks in Windows 10:

Right-click on the Network Icon in the system tray and select the "Open Network and Sharing Center" option.

In the Control Panel desktop app that appears, click the network whose password you want to access. The network should appear as a link that's next to the Connections field.

Now, under the Connection section, click on the "Wireless Properties" button to display the wireless network properties.

Navigate to "Security tab" and click on the "Show characters" so you access the password.

How to use the Wi-Fi Sense

The Windows 10 OS is shipped with a new network feature that's called the Wi-Fi Sense. The Wi-Fi Sense is basically a feature that lets your computer connect automatically to Wi-Fi networks that your friends and other acquaintances have hitherto attached to.

Now, here is the most interesting thing about the Wi-Fi Sense: it allows your computer to connect to wireless networks that your friends have been connecting to even if you don't have the password for that network. Doesn't this scare you?

Well, you shouldn't be worried. By default, the Wi-Fi Sense cannot share any Wi-Fi passwords with anyone else that has joined the network. In fact, for every network that you join, you'll, first of all, be asked if you want to share it with your friends on social networks or not. If you agree, then the Wi-Fi Sense will share it. Otherwise, the feature will remain anonymous.

Now, with that information clarified, let's dive in and find out how you can use the Wi-Fi Sense in Windows 10:

To connect to free and other open hotspot networks, ensure that you click on the "On" position that's placed under the "Connect to networks shared by my contacts."

You should be aware that not all the Wi-Fi networks you connect to are secure.

To share a particular network connection with your friends and acquaintances, ensure that you click on the "On" position that's placed under the "Connect to networks shared by my contacts."

On the same note, if you want to stop sharing a particular wireless network, then you can just click on the "Stop Sharing" button for that particular wireless network.

How to manage IP Addresses Assignment in Windows 10

Sometimes when establishing your home network it's simpler to assign each PC its own IP address rather than using the DHCP—Dynamic Host Configuration Protocol. When you use the DHCP, each PC will request and be assigned an IP address every time it's turned on.

Troubleshooting such networks is very tedious because you can't remember their IP addresses.

On the other hand, if you're using the Static IP approach to assign IP addresses, then you'll prevent IP address conflicts that may arise between devices. This provides you with ample opportunity to manage them. While the process of assigning IP addresses to Windows PC's is essentially the same, getting to where you need when assigning the IP addresses can be quite tricky.

Let's dive in and find out how you can assign IP address using the static method in Windows 10:

On the start menu, type *"**network and sharing**"* into the Search box and hit the enter key.

From the results of the search process, click on the *"**Network and Sharing Center**."*

From the left pane of your Network and Sharing Center click on "**Change adapter settings**."

Now, Right-click on the name of your local adapter and select the "Properties."

From the Local Area Connection Properties window that appears select the "**Internet Protocol Version 4 (TCP/IPv4)**."

Click on the "**Properties**" button.

Select the radio button and enter the correct IP address, the Subnet mask, and the right Default gateway that matches your network setup. You should also enter the right Preferred and Alternate DNS server addresses.

Once you've entered the correct IP Address settings, check the "Validate settings upon exit" so that Windows can find any issues with the addresses that you've you entered. When you've completed, don't forget to click the

OK button.

Close your Local Area Connections Window.

How to Use the Registry Editor to Manage Hardware and Software Issues in Windows 10

If you want to become an advanced Windows 10 user, you should know how to use a registry editor. A registry editor can help you to manage most –if not all—of your software and hardware issues. Knowing how to use a registry in Windows 10 will go a long way in helping you to understand Windows 10 OS. In fact understanding, the structure of registry editor in Windows 10 is a surefire to solving most problems across all the Windows OS.

To start, let's begin by defining what a registry editor is.

A Registry Editor is a basic tool that's intended for advanced users to help view and change settings in the computer's registry. A registry is a collection of all the information that makes a computer run efficiently. All the

Window OS's—Windows 10 included— use the registry as

a reference point when updating and making changes to

your system.

The Registry in any computer system has two essential

elements. These elements are the keys and the values.

The Registry keys behave like container objects and are

similar to the folders on your computer. On the other

hand, the Registry values are the non-container objects.

They are similar to files on your computer. Now, the

Registry Keys may contain values, or they can have extra

keys.

The Registry Keys are referenced with a syntax that's

similar to the Windows' path names. In fact, we use the

backslashes (\) to indicate the levels of hierarchy in the

Keys. On the same note, the Keys should be case insensitive names that don't have backslashes.

The hierarchy of the keys can be accessed from a known root key handle. A root key handle can be anonymous. However, its effective value should be constant integrated handle—which can be mapped to the content of the Registry key that's preloaded by the kernel from DLL

For instance, the key "HKEY_LOCAL_MACHINE\Software\Microsoft\Windows" can be interpreted as "Windows" which is a subkey of the "Microsoft" which is a subkey of "Software." The root key, in this case, becomes "HKEY_LOCAL_MACHINE." Got it?

Now, there are 7 predefined root keys in the Registry. These root key are named according to their constant handles which are defined in the Win32 API. Here are the seven root keys in the registry:

- HKEY_LOCAL_MACHINE

- HKEY_CLASSES_ROOT or HKCR

- HKEY_CURRENT_CONFIG or HKCC

- HKEY_USERS or HKU

- HKEY_PERFORMANCE_DATA

- HKEY_CURRENT_USER or HKCU

A Registry Editor can help you make changes to your computer. Such changes include installing new programs, creating user profiles or even adding new hardware devices. So, a Registry Editor should let you view your registry folders, the files and other settings for each registry file in a computer.

It's important to note that advanced users should only use Registry Editors. This is because it contains complex system information that's necessary for healthy functioning of a computer. Now, any incorrect change to the registry can render your computer inoperable. As a precaution, it's important to ensure you've backed up the registry before you attempt to change any setting.

How to Open the Registry Editor

Here's is how the Registry Editor can be opened:

- Click on the start button, type "Run" in the search button and hit the enter key.

- Now, in the Run window that appears type "*regedit*" and hit the enter key.

- Your Registry Editor will open. Just make sure you confirm or type your Administrator password when asked in the confirmation window.

Alternatively, here's how you can start the Registry Editor:

- Press the Windows Key + R.

- In the Run window that appears type *"regedit"* and hit the enter key.

- Your Registry Editor will open. Just make sure you confirm or type your Administrator password when asked in the confirmation window.

How to use the Registry Editor to manage software and hardware issues

So, how can use the Registry Editor to manage software and hardware issues on your PC?

Well, a Registry Editor can be used to control the following components in Windows 10:

- The System Hardware

- The Installed Software and Drivers

- The System Settings

- The Profile Information

Your system hardware includes all the physical devices that have been connected to your computer. This may include the mice, the keyboard, the printers and hard disks just to mention but a few. All the information about these hardware devices will be kept in the Registry Editor according to their Keys and entries.

The installed software and Drivers refer to all the information about all the applications that you've installed on your PC and their Registry Keys and their entries. On the other hand, the drivers are applications for that ensures the hardware devices connected to your computer are running smoothly. All their Registry Keys and entries are stored in the installed software and drivers.

The system settings contain all the information about your PC. This includes the type of OS you're using— whether it's a 32-bit or 64-bit—and other hardware device's information such as the system clock's speed, the RAM capacity and Hard Disk capacity, just to mention but a few.

The last components that will be contained in a Registry Editor are the Profile Information. The profile information provides all the information about personal data that's associated with a particular user on a computer. The profile information has a customized desktop environment for each user in Windows 10. So, if you wish to change a particular profile for a user, then you can use the Registry Editor.

Let's dive in and find out how you can use the Registry Editor to manage these components.

#1: How to restore a computer using the Registry Editor

In this example, we explain how you can use the Registry Editor to help you restore your computer.

Here's how you can restore your Windows 10:

- Boot Windows 10 into Safe Mode (This will protect your vital files and drivers). For you to boot into Safe Mode, press F8 on your keyboard while you turning on your computer.

- This will trigger the boot options. Locate the "Safe Mode" and press the enter key.

- Once the computer has booted, Click on the start button, type "Run" in the search button and hit the enter key.

- Now, in the Run window that appears type "*regedit*" and hit the enter key.

- Your Registry Editor will open. Just make sure you confirm or type your Administrator password when asked in the confirmation window.

- click on the File menu in the window that appears.

- Click on "Import" menu.

- Now, in the Import Registry dialogue box, browse to find the location where you saved your backup file.

- Once you've found the backup file, click on "Open" in the Look In Folders dialog box.

#2: How to uninstall a program using the Registry Editor

For every application that's installed on your computer, there's an uninstall entry that's stored in the Registry. The uninstall entries for all the applications are grouped under the uninstall entry in the Registry. So, if you want to remove an application in Windows 10, then you should look for the uninstall entries in the Registry.

Here are steps that can help you to remove an application using the Registry Editor:

- Click on the start button, type "Run" in the search button and hit the enter key.
- Now, in the Run window that appears type "*regedit*" and hit the enter key.

- Your Registry Editor will open. Just make sure you confirm or type your Administrator password when asked in the confirmation window.

- Locate   the "HKEY_LOCAL_MACHINE\Software\currentversion\ Uninstall" entry in the Registry Editor's window.

- Select the application that you wish to uninstall in the left pane of your Window.

- Now select the program's "uninstallstring" and double click on it.

- Copy that string of the value data.

- On the start button, type "Run" button and hit the enter key.

- Now, in the Run window that appears paste the string that you had copied earlier and hit the enter key.

- Wait for the uninstallation process to complete.

- Reboot your PC.

#3: How to Remove Device Driver using the Registry Editor

If your hardware devices stop working, and you find that re-installing it using the Devices and Printers isn't working, then you can uninstall it using the Registry Editor. This will require that you delete the driver from the Registry Editor. Once you've removed the driver, you can install the device driver again.

Here's an example of how a printer driver can be removed in Windows 10:

- Click on the start menu, type "Run" in the search button and hit the enter key.

- Now, in the Run window that appears type "*regedit*" and hit the enter key.

- Your Registry Editor will open. Just make sure you confirm or type your Administrator password when asked in the confirmation window.

- Now, navigate through the keys "HKEY_LOCAL_MACHINE\ SYSTEM\CurrentControlSet\ Control \Print\Environments\Drivers\Version-3."

- Right-click the name of the printer from the left pane of your Window and click"Delete" option from the context menu that appears.

- Click "Yes" command when prompted.

- Now go back to "Print" key again and expand the "Printers" key.

- Right-click on the name of the printer from the left pane of your Window.

- Click "Delete" command and then the "Yes" command to launch the uninstallation process.

- Choose the start menu, and type "services.msc" in the search field and hit press the Enter key.

- Double click on the "Print Spooler" and click the "Stop" button.

- Click on "Start" to restart the printing service.

Conclusion

Windows used to be famous for its instability, but (since Windows 7, at least) that it is no longer a problem. In my tests, the operating system behaved in a uniform fashion. The performance did not suffer and was always quick.

The interface seems to be right on the spot. Anyone who has used Windows can use Windows 10 without problem, it is a familiar experience, designed to make the most of the keyboard and mouse. Whoever comes from Windows 7 is not going to need to learn anything to start working, but can explore the new features and discover tools that can serve him better. That is the balance that any operating system should strive to achieve.

The elements and principles to use Windows are the same. But Microsoft made some improvements. It not only added the window docking options that were in Windows 8, but also improved Alt + Tab and made faster switching applications. It also included the option of multiple desktops, which allow you to use different programs in separate spaces: you can have one with Excel and mail while you work, and one with Steam and Spotify for your leisure hours. It really is not a necessary option, but good for decluttering.

Tablet mode:

But Windows 10 does not leave everything intact: Microsoft added touches of Metro where they were needed, and was very careful not to damage the

experience. They returned some of the ideas of his

predecessor, as the window docking or tablet mode. But

unlike Windows 8, all these elements feel quite integrated

into a single experience.

The new start menu is perhaps the most iconic change,

and is fine. It can be used like Windows 7, scanning a list

of apps and services. But it can also turn into a customized

startup screen to navigate tiled and a touch screen.

In addition, the search bar lets you access any part of the

operating system without diving in the control panel, or in

a menu of applications. It is, in fact, the best way to do it:

it is very fast. On the other hand, Windows 10 is quite

careful with notifications. If the user wants, he can see the notification bar, but they do not usually interfere.

The tablet mode is basically an input screen like Windows 8 was supposed to be, designed for touch devices, but can be used on any PC.

All these changes seem designed with a premise: "everything in its place '. It is clear that Microsoft took a keen interest in the fluidity of user. IAs far as I could try, Windows 10 worked without annoying.

The ecosystem

In windows 8 there were many stores and different versions of apps; and confusion discouraged many to use. Windows 10 tries various solutions: from removing all technical barriers to port apps from other platforms, to puting a direct link to the store in the browser, so any search results returned from the app store.

But the problem is still there. The store is full of apps for 'tablet' mode, and very few for the desktop mode. So, Windows will not get better download apps from the store from the manufacturer's website, so that PC users still have no reason to explore.

In fact, many of the most popular apps are not even at the store: iTunes, Spotify, Firefox, Pidgin ... and those other, largely, are not convincing; They seem bad copies, or are uncertain or suspicious versions directly. If Microsoft wants to consolidate Windows and ecosystem still has much work to do.

USERS HAVE LITTLE REASON TO OPEN THE WINDOWS STORE

Universal apps -those that can be used on PCs, mobile phones and other screens-, meanwhile, began to come preinstalled on your operating system: maps, weather and photos are anymore. Your browsing responds to the screen size, and generally fulfill their promise.

Another big bet with Microsoft Windows 10 is to get what I call the 'snowball effect'. This is achieved when the value obtained by the user to use a service increases when another product or service from the same manufacturer is used. Or, to put it in another way: Office, onedrive, OneNote or Skype work better when Windows 10 is used, and vice versa.

Windows 10 side, it is implemented flawlessly: OneNote and onedrive are implemented throughout the operating system, Skype contacts are synchronized with the native email and calendar apps and integration with Xbox has good ideas.

But the only way to make the experience complete is that users also prefer Microsoft products on their phones, and that is something that can only be achieved in one of these ways: getting people to migrate en masse to Windows Phone, or having these all features in iOS and Android. Will have to see if the strategy works.

Two of blockbuster news from Windows 10 are Cortana and Edge. The personal assistant is character-modeled: i.e. it is supposed to learn user habits and the more you know, the more sensible and personalized it help you.

Within what can be done, it works great. It is agile, quite human and has a sense of humor. Its interaction is fluid and integrates well with the OS and other apps such as email or calendar. It is useful at times, but in principle does nothing very different from Siri or Google Now.

It is initially optimized for use in English, and precisely the United States English. This not only puts a language barrier, but also removes many functions of geographical location. Even talking in that language, in Latin America its database of restaurants is not very good, and will be difficult to alert you when you go to your next appointment on time.

Microsoft said this year would support Cortana to more countries, so the wizard will not only learn French, Japanese and Spanish but also show them its full potential users of that country. But for now, we must have a little patience.

Draw on the websites.

Edge, meanwhile, lacks a clear-cut advantage. Its engine is a fast specimen and loads fast for most sites, but not all. Its performance is quite accomplished, and it appears that it will eventually shake off the burdens that dragged Internet Explorer.

But I had to stop using it. There are web tools that are not well understood, and one of those is the platform I use to feed the contents of my career as a writer. Their main argument is its integration with Cortana, and that allows handwritten notes and share sites. And although the former is well-designed also suffering from the geographic-restrictions, the latter is not very convincing.

The annotation tool is basic but does the job. It allows you to cut, draw and highlight on websites; export the result and share it on social networks. A specific niche, such as designers, or those working in digital products, will find there is a reason to change. But that same can be done with an extension of Chrome or Firefox.

And that is the point. There is no reason for people to switch to Edge. While download and install another browser takes a minute more and the result is impeccable, switching to the new 'browser' is not as wasteful as having to export configurations, passwords and Bookmarks-, but could affect the workflow of some users because there are tools that do not yet work well there.

Therefore, we still cannot recommend mass. It is a good attempt and an option that will satisfy basic users, but who need a browser that works with it or do anything that puts should still use a traditional, like Chrome or Firefox.

Finally, another good Windows 10 promise is Continuum. This function allows you to keep your workspace on any machine with just log on to your Windows account. It's really useful: I could get into my home PC and continue my work. However, its setting is not immediate, so it is not a viable option for when the user is in a rush option.

Windows 10 and Xbox One

Windows 10

The perfect couple?

Xbox is integrated into Windows 10 with three functions: a social network where you can see the achievements of your friends, a tool to create and share videos of your plays, and the most interesting: an option to play on the Xbox from the PC using streaming.

In our tests, streaming experience was frustrating. The connection between the computer and the console is not easy to do, even in a network without congestion.

Furthermore, it requires the player to have a gamepad connected to your PC; and if you only have one, you must disconnect the Xbox and this complicates things a bit.

PC XBOX PROMISES, BUT COULD IMPROVE

When you can finally see your Xbox One on the screen of your computer, the connection is unstable and sometimes when that happens, the picture is full of interruptions. In a game that requires fast movements, it is deadly. Maybe a new router will make things work better. But this tool still has a long way to be the 'trump card' that Microsoft is touting.

Moreover, the tool for making videos has the same problem. It is easy to see that it is a good idea: with the explosion of streaming video game, Microsoft wants to make it easier for users to create their own material and avoid having to resort to third-party tools (in addition to promoting the inexhaustible source of free advertising).

Windows 10

Does it pass the test?

The answer is yes. Casual users will find that the operating system is more flexible than ever, allowing them to be very productive. The 'power users' will find the same freedoms as ever, and improved stability.

To both users, the experience is solid and the interface is well designed. Those already living in Windows feel safe in familiar territory, but better. Microsoft managed to achieve a very difficult point: the new Windows will feel new and also importantly familiar.

MICROSOFT DID NOT DO EVERYTHING RIGHT, BUT I GOT THE MOST IMPORTANT

But there are problems. The ecosystem improved somewhat, but still has difficulties. Cortana is formidable, Edge still lags behind. Integration with Xbox is a good promise, but still is not a reality that works quite well.

This shows that Microsoft did not do everything right, but it got the most important part: to offer a good place to give their users a centralized digital life. And the future is promising: as in all operating systems, while Windows 10 will only be getting better. It is likely that now that Windows XP is dead: Microsoft just created the most important Windows in its history.

One can still experience the pleasure of interface changes brought about by windows 10 and will continue doing so in the considerable future. I hope this book has been able to get a good picture of what Microsoft offered in this OS. Please let me know what additional content would be helpful to learn about for users that can be added to the book.